American JAZZ
DIZZY GILLESPIE

MARY BOONE

Mitchell Lane
PUBLISHERS

P.O. Box 196
Hockessin, Delaware 19707

American JAZZ

Benny Goodman

Bessie Smith

Billie Holiday

Charlie Parker

Count Basie

Dizzy Gillespie

Louis Armstrong

Miles Davis

Ornette Coleman

Scott Joplin

Copyright © 2013 by Mitchell Lane Publishers

PUBLISHER'S NOTE: The facts on which this book is based have been thoroughly researched. Documentation of such research can be found on page 44. While every possible effort has been made to ensure accuracy, the publisher will not assume liability for damages caused by inaccuracies in the data, and makes no warranty on the accuracy of the information contained herein.

Printing 1 2 3 4 5 6 7 8 9

**Library of Congress
Cataloging-in-Publication Data**

Boone, Mary, 1963–
 Dizzy Gillespie / by Mary Boone.
    p. cm. — (American jazz)
 Includes bibliographical references and index.
 ISBN 978-1-61228-272-5 (library bound)
 1. Gillespie, Dizzy, 1917–1993—Juvenile literature. 2. Jazz musicians—United States—Biography—Juvenile literature. 3. Bop (Music)—History and criticism—Juvenile literature. I. Title.
 ML3930.G47B66 2013
 788.9'2165092—dc23
 [B]
                                                    2012008630

eBook ISBN: 9781612283487

                                                            PLB

Contents

Chapter **1**

A Turbulent Childhood

During the 1920s, cotton was planted on most of the farmland along the North Carolina–South Carolina border. Cotton was king, and wealthy white farmers paid blacks less than a dollar a day to fill canvas sacks with the soft, fluffy fibers.

On a sweltering summer day in 1928, John Gillespie joined his brother Wesley in this rite of passage. He crawled through the rows on his hands and knees, pricking his fingers on the sharp prongs that held the cotton inside the boll. The dust made him cough until tears flowed from his eyes, and the heat made him nauseous. He took water breaks and went back to picking, only to feel sick within minutes.

At the end of that day of picking, Wesley had gathered 125 pounds of cotton and earned 60 cents for his efforts. John's harvest weighed a measly 15 pounds, earning him just 8 cents.

Years later, John "Dizzy" Gillespie told a newspaper reporter that it was on that hot summer day that he marched home and told his mother: "I wasn't cut out for picking cotton. Someday I'm gonna be a musician and you'll be proud of me."[1]

His boast may have seemed far-fetched at the time, but his forecast was accurate. The boy who failed as a farmhand grew up to become one of the most recognizable and popular figures in jazz history.

John Birks Gillespie (the nickname "Dizzy" came about much later) was born in Cheraw, South Carolina, on October 21, 1917. He was the youngest of James Penfield Gillespie and Lottie Powe Gillespie's nine children.

James Gillespie was a bricklayer and amateur bandleader who passed his love of music on to his son. Even when money was tight, James saved his pennies to buy instruments. The family had a drum set, upright piano, clarinet, guitar, mandolin, and bass fiddle. James taught himself how to play all the instruments, and he was thrilled that, by age three, his youngest son was already exploring melodies on the piano and rhythmic patterns on the drums.

John was a very active boy, playing games, climbing trees, telling jokes, and playing music. The first adult who tried to channel his energy was a neighbor named Amanda Harrington. Mrs. Harrington was a retired schoolteacher who allowed John to play her piano and eat ice cream while she taught him how to read and count. The boy was bright and had learned so much in Mrs. Harrington's informal preschool that he was bored when he actually began school. His boredom caused him to get into mischief—until he met Alice Wilson, his third grade teacher. She appreciated his musical talent and tolerated his restlessness.

John's father died in 1927, following a severe asthma attack. After his death, John became even more rebellious. His mother became a seamstress, but her earnings weren't enough to keep his family from plummeting deep into poverty.

By 1929, John had become both frustrated and embarrassed by his circumstances. But that all changed when Miss Wilson visited John's fifth grade classroom to ask if any students might like to join a band.

John was the youngest recruit in the Robert Smalls School's new band, so he got last choice of instruments: a trombone that Miss Wilson feared he was too small to play. John insisted that, even with arms so short that he couldn't extend the trombone's slide to the farthest position, he could learn to play it.

The eleven-year-old practiced nonstop and improved steadily. Soon he was recruited to play in a smaller, five-piece band. A year later, Miss Wilson found John an old cornet to play instead of the trombone.

When he was twelve, John performed with Miss Wilson's band at the school's minstrel show. It was his first taste of performing in public, and he loved it.

Shortly after that show, John's musical world was rocked when he learned that Miss Wilson's own musical skills were so limited that she couldn't read music and only played in the key of B-flat. When John was challenged to play in another musical key, he failed miserably. He could have given up. Instead, he vowed to practice even more and began taking lessons from his cousin Norman Powe.

Recognizing her musical shortcomings, Miss Wilson dropped out of the group but continued to support the Robert Smalls School band. She found a trumpet for John to play and helped the group add a bassist, a clarinetist/saxophonist, and a singer for their first paying job—a dance at a white school. The band was a hit and soon began booking parties and dances in nearby towns.

The band's popularity lasted several years, until 1931 when their trombonist, a young man named Bill McNeil, was lynched. A mob believed he had been peeking into white girls' windows without their knowledge. It wasn't clear how he died, but according to Gillespie's memoirs, the rumor was a mob had put the teenager on the railroad tracks in front of a train.[2] His murder underscored the divide between blacks and whites in the southern United States at the time. John's cousin Norman took McNeil's place in the band, but it was never the same.

By 1933, Dizzy faced some difficult decisions. He was about to graduate from Robert Smalls School (at the time, ninth grade was the highest public school grade available to Cheraw's black children). He wanted to perform professionally but was wise enough to know he'd have to pick cotton or do hard labor to help support himself. That's when a young music fan named Catherine McKay stepped in and, ultimately, changed his life.

McKay was a student at the Laurinburg Institute, a co-ed black boarding school in North Carolina. Laurinburg had two top-notch bands that played around the region and raised large amounts of

money for the school. McKay asked the school to replace its graduating trumpet player and trombonist with John and Norman. Neither boy could have afforded to attend the school on his own, but thanks to McKay's support, both were awarded full scholarships.

Laurinburg provided John with the opportunity to improve his musical skills. He played with both the school orchestra and the marching band, and he spent summers working on the school's farm. Music was his passion but he didn't spend much time on his other coursework. Instead of studying, he busied himself playing pranks and getting into fights.

John's mother and two of his siblings moved to Philadelphia in March 1935. John wanted to go along but his mother insisted he stay in North Carolina and graduate from Laurinburg. With his family more than 500 miles away, John got depressed. He skipped classes and paid even less attention to his homework. He failed a class his final semester. Faced with the possibility of having to retake the course, he decided to quit school.

A neighbor offered him a ride to Philadelphia and he accepted. He'd grown up at Laurinburg, and he felt ready to strike out on his own as a professional musician. More than anything, John wanted to make good on his promise to make his mother "proud of me."[3]

The Laurinburg Institute

Dizzy Gillespie's alma mater, the Laurinburg Institute, is the United States' oldest historically black prep school. Emmanuel Monty and Tinny McDuffie started the school in 1904 with the dream of providing quality education and guidance for black children, many of whom would not otherwise have been able to attend school. The leadership of the school remained in the McDuffie family through three generations. Frank H. McDuffie Sr., son of Emmanuel and Tinny, was president from 1953 to 1990. Frank H. "Bishop" McDuffie Jr. became the school's president in 1991.

Sam Jones

Laurinburg has long been recognized for producing outstanding basketball players; NBA players Sam Jones (who in 1957 was one of the first African Americans drafted by the NBA, or National Basketball Association), Jerrod Mustaf, and Charlie Scott are among its graduates. However, the school's gymnasium was condemned in the late 1990s. After that, Laurinburg teams had to practice on public park courts. Despite this hardship, the school maintained its reputation in basketball.

In 2009, the NCAA declared that the school had "not cleared" a review of its academics and curriculum. (The NCAA—the National Collegiate Athletic Association—protects athletes while they are in college, which includes making sure they receive a good education.) Without clearance, Laurinburg graduates would not be eligible for athletic scholarships. Laurinburg administrators say they remain true to their mission to provide excellence in education. In 2010, even though the small school had only six full-time faculty members, McDuffie said that 80 percent of its graduates had gone on to complete college "on time."[4]

Making a Name for Himself

When John Gillespie arrived in Philadelphia, he became the seventh resident in his family's tiny apartment. He, his mother, some siblings, and their spouses shared a hodgepodge of cots, couches, and mattresses, with no one getting much privacy or sleep.

Eager to both earn some cash and make his mark on the city's music scene, Gillespie set out with a $13 trumpet stuffed into a brown paper bag to audition at neighborhood saloons and bars. He quickly landed a job at a bar called the Green Gate Inn, where he earned $8 per week (equal to approximately $132 in 2012). After just a month of playing at the rowdy Green Gate, he got another job offer, this one for $12 per week, and Gillespie decided to join the musician's union.

It didn't take long for local musicians to begin talking about the area's newest trumpet player. Soon, Frankie Fairfax, who led one of Philadelphia's best bands at the time, contacted him and offered him a tryout.

Gillespie was used to reading musical notation, but when he got to the audition he saw music like none he'd ever seen before. Notes were written in pencil; a pencil line across a note meant it was an eighth note, and an eighth rest was just a straight line.

"Guys had gotten used to reading this bad notation, and when I got up there and they put that music up before me, I started playing eighth rests for notes, sixteenth rests for notes—everything just came out wrong," Gillespie wrote in his memoir *To Be, or Not . . . To Bop.* "It ended up with them thinking that I couldn't read music and they wouldn't give me the job."[1]

Almost worse than not getting the job was having pianist Bill Doggett make fun of his playing. "That little dizzy cat's from down South," Gillespie recalled Doggett saying, "carries his horn around in a paper bag. You know he can't read."[2] It was the first time someone had called him Dizzy, but that wouldn't be his nickname until later.

Although he was heartbroken not to have landed the job, he quickly found work with other area bands. Before long, a disagreement over money tore apart Frankie Fairfax's band, and the players quit. When Fairfax organized another band in November 1935, Gillespie finally got the big band job he was hoping for, playing in the trumpet section alongside Palmer "Fats" Davis and others.

One day before rehearsal, Gillespie was playing the piano when Davis pulled up a chair so that he could listen to his fellow band member. Soon others gathered, tapping their toes along to Gillespie's piano playing. By the time he finished playing, most of the other musicians had made their way to their seats.

Dizzy recalled the scene in his book *To Be, or Not . . . To Bop*:

> Fats Palmer looked across at my empty seat in the trumpet section and cracked a joke. "Where's Dizzy, man?" Everybody started laughing. [Drummer] Norman Dibbles said, "Yeah, that's a good name for that cat!" My name has been Dizzy to everybody, ever since; even my wife calls me that.[3]

Fairfax's band played weekly shows at the ritzy Strand Ballroom and an occasional gig at resorts in Pennsylvania. The group took a five-week leave of absence to go on tour with nationally known bandleader and popular vocalist Tiny Bradshaw.

Because of the size of the tour—which took them through Maryland; Washington, D.C.; Virginia; and the Carolinas—band members thought they had achieved stardom. After all, instead of piling into a couple of beat-up old cars, they were traveling in a Greyhound bus and had both a road manager and a valet.

The first two weeks of the tour were successful, but when they reached Richmond, Virginia, the situation fell apart fast. Several shows were canceled and, without money for a hotel, band members were forced to sleep on the bus. When they did get a gig, the fourteen men shared two hotel rooms, sleeping in shifts, three or four in the bed crosswise.

The musicians returned to Philadelphia both wiser and wearier. As Fairfax worked to reorganize his band, he hired two top-notch New York trumpeters: Charlie Shavers and Carl "Bama" Warwick.

Gillespie, Shavers, and Warwick became good friends, hanging out socially and learning from each other musically. Shavers was a diehard fan of trumpeter Roy Eldridge, having memorized many of Eldridge's solos. Gillespie loved learning about Eldridge's improvisational techniques, and the band mates learned to use some of his stylings in their performances. As a result, the Fairfax band thrived.

Trumpeter Charlie Shavers (left) introduced Gillespie to the improvisational stylings of Roy Eldridge.

Tiny Bradshaw was one of the most prominent jazz and rhythm and blues bandleaders of the 1930s and 1940s.

In 1936, the group continued its shows at the Strand and other Philadelphia clubs. It also took its show on the road, traveling to nearby clubs in Pennsylvania, New Jersey, Maryland, and Delaware.

In the fall of 1936, Tiny Bradshaw convinced Shavers and Warwick to join his band. They wanted their pal Dizzy to come along, but he didn't want to leave his family behind. Shavers and Warwick eventually left Tiny Bradshaw for better-paying gigs with Lucky Millinder's orchestra in New York City. They thought they'd convinced Millinder to hire Gillespie to replace the group's third trumpet player, so Gillespie moved to New York in March 1937. He got a couple weeks' pay from Millinder but never actually performed with the group because Millinder was not willing to fire his other trumpet player.

Playing for a big-time New York City group was every musician's dream. Gillespie's pride wouldn't allow him to return to Philadelphia, so he worked hard and picked up jobs where he could. In April 1937, he heard that bandleader Teddy Hill was looking for a new trumpet player; Gillespie auditioned wearing gloves and an overcoat. His flashiness upset several of the band's members, who lobbied against hiring him. Hill, however, decided to give Gillespie the job. Soon Gillespie was making $45 per week while playing with Hill's band in the United States. When the group toured Europe, he brought home $70 per week.

Gillespie had made it—big time.

Roy Eldridge

Also known as "Little Jazz," Roy David
Eldridge was a fiery trumpeter who was
short in stature with a larger-than-life
stage presence. Born January 30, 1911,
in Pittsburgh, Pennsylvania, Eldridge got
his earliest training from his older
brother Joe, an alto saxophonist. Before
taking up the trumpet, Roy played the
drums, a fact many music historians
believe contributed to the great rhythmic
drive of his music.

At age sixteen, Eldridge began
performing professionally, playing drums,
trumpet, and tuba for a touring carnival.
A few years later, he began playing for bandleaders including
Fletcher Henderson, Gene Krupa, and Artie Shaw. Eventually he
began recording under his own name. He also gained a reputation
as a bandleader, forming an eight-man group in Chicago in 1936.

Over the years, he performed as a soloist with a wide array
of swing bands, including the Gene Krupa Band and the Artie
Shaw Band. Eldridge toured briefly with Benny Goodman and
took up residence in Paris in 1950, where he made some of his
most successful recordings. He returned to New York in 1951
and continued freelancing with small bands, including work with
Coleman Hawkins, Benny Carter, Ella Fitzgerald, and Johnny
Hodges.

Eldridge suffered a stroke in 1980 and was no longer able to
play the trumpet. He did, however, continue to make music as a
singer and pianist, performing until his death in 1989.

Chapter **3**

The Birth of Bebop

Gillespie quickly learned that, while he was skilled at reading music and improvising, he needed to work on things like playing in unison with other brass players and learning to sustain long tones. He later credited fellow Teddy Hill band trumpeter Bill Dillard with tutoring him in the fine points of big band performance.

The Hill group was a first-rate band that played to full houses wherever it went. In spring 1937, the band joined with several other acts to form the Cotton Club Revue, an extravaganza that included bands, vocalists, dancers, and acrobats. The revue was scheduled to perform for six weeks in Paris with, perhaps, more European dates to follow. The show received rave reviews and drew huge crowds eager to see dancers perform the energetic Lindy Hop. After Paris, the show moved into the London Palladium for a five-week engagement. The revue completed its tour with shows in Dublin, Ireland, and Manchester, England.

Upon returning to New York in September 1937, Gillespie got news that his trip to Europe had violated a seldom-enforced rule about transferring from one city's union to another. As punishment, he was limited to one-night shows in New York or short out-of-town tours. He was also banned from steady employment with Hill or any other band for ninety days. The penalty made it tough for Gillespie to earn money, but it also had a positive impact on both his personal and professional

FOR THE FIRST TIME IN ANY COUNTRY OUTSIDE NEW YORK
THE AUTHENTIC
COTTON CLUB REVUE
IN ITS ENTIRETY
AT THE
LONDON
PALLADIUM
JULY 26th
FOR A SHORT
SEASON

THE FASTEST
ENTERTAINMENT
IN THE WORLD BY
60 OF
HARLEM'S FOREMOST
ENTERTAINERS
THE AUTHENTIC
COTTON CLUB REVUE
LONDON PALLADIUM   JULY 26th
Orchestral accompaniment under the direction of TEDDY HILL

Sixty of Harlem's most famous entertainers took their fast-paced show to Europe in 1937 as the Cotton Club Revue. Gillespie, who was in the Teddy Hill Band at the time, was part of the show.

lives. While he was serving out his penalty, Gillespie met Lorraine Willis, a beautiful dancer from Washington, D.C., and the two began dating.

During this time, Gillespie became entrenched in two movements that forever changed the sound and feel of jazz music: bebop and the Afro-Cuban revolution.

While scrounging for work, Gillespie began working with drummer Kenny "Klook" Clarke. The two developed rhythms that would eventually become the foundation for bebop. Another friend, trumpeter Mario Bauzá, helped Gillespie find work with salsa bands in East Harlem. Hearing the intricate percussion patterns that came from conga drums, bongo drums, and timbale drums inspired him to explore his African heritage. The impulsive, pulsating rhythms inspired him to play with even more freedom. He created musical phrases that began and ended in unexpected places, phrases that varied in length and intensity.

Instead of words, scat performers sang along in nonsensical syllables: *mah-na-mah, boodely, eeba, oobop-sha-bam.* Gillespie was no longer constrained by steady swing band rhythms. He was creating something new and exciting.

By 1939, Clarke and Gillespie were both playing with the Teddy Hill Band. They were able to try out their new sound at the New York World's Fair, where their band performed ten shows per day. The group backed a Lindy Hopper dance troupe at the Savoy Pavilion, a temporary version of Harlem's Savoy Ballroom. Audiences there experienced a style of music that was notably different from swing; notes were no

Gillespie, who writes a phrase of bebop music, is credited with helping to lay the groundwork for this fast-tempo genre. Bebop is defined by its blend of harmonic structure, intricate rhythms, and melody.

longer confined by bars and counts, and rhythm ruled supreme. Unfortunately, Hill's musicians weren't as thrilled with the World's Fair shows; in spite of a demanding schedule, the men were paid far less than normal. When Hill complained to the union, the whole group was fired—from the fair and from the Savoy Ballroom. Gillespie found himself looking for work once again.

This time, however, dancer Lorraine Willis took an interest in helping him find a job. She was beginning to care deeply for Gillespie but couldn't imagine marrying him if he didn't have steady work. She asked her friends to recommend Gillespie to Cab Calloway, leader of one of the best-paying bands in the country. Fortunately, Calloway appreciated Gillespie's talents and added him to his band in August 1939. Less than a month after joining the group, a nervous Gillespie debuted his bebop concepts in his first recorded solo. A second recording session, this one set up by jazz great Lionel Hampton, took place three months later. Gillespie's more confident-sounding solo was notable enough that it

Cab Calloway was an energetic showman, bandleader, singer, actor, and trendsetting fashion plate. By the late 1930s, his band was one of the top grossing acts in jazz and became a proving ground for many young musicians, including Gillespie, Ben Webster, Cozy Cole, and Doc Cheatham.

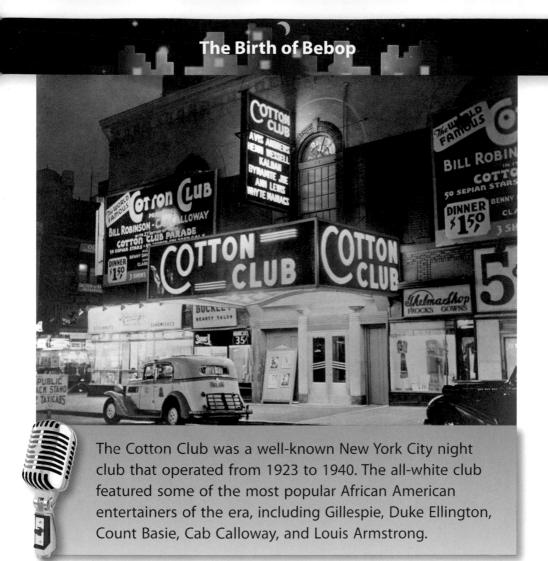

The Cotton Club was a well-known New York City night club that operated from 1923 to 1940. The all-white club featured some of the most popular African American entertainers of the era, including Gillespie, Duke Ellington, Count Basie, Cab Calloway, and Louis Armstrong.

earned him his first mention by a big-time American music publication. A reviewer for *Metronome* wrote: "Gillespie emits some neat muted trumpeting on 'Hot Mallets.' "[1] Bebop's lightning-fast tempos and spirited improvisations were beginning to draw notice and praise.

The success spilled over into his private life. He and Lorraine married in 1940. Their marriage would last for 53 years.

It was during the Lionel Hampton recording session that Gillespie became friends with guitarist Charlie Christian. Christian's ability to move effortlessly between sharply different rhythmic patterns made for music that was free flowing and unpredictable. The two began playing together at nightclubs all over New York City, often joined by drummer Kenny Clarke. The three often ended up at a Manhattan after-hours

Dizzy Gillespie's wife, Lorraine Willis Gillespie, admired her husband's talents. She jokingly plugs her ears while he plays.

club run by Charlie Monroe. Shows there wouldn't get started until around 4 A.M.; on occasion, jazz stars including trumpeter Hot Lips Page, bassist Jimmy Blanton, and saxophonist Don Byas would sit in with the young musicians (Gillespie was only in his early twenties at the time). The informal jam sessions attracted large crowds of hip music lovers, both black and white, and often lasted until 7 A.M.

The late-late-night jam sessions could have exhausted Gillespie, but instead they invigorated him, providing a break from the precisely written music he was often paid to play. Innovation and creativity were fueling his music, and his audiences enjoyed it all.

Lorraine Willis

Lorraine Willis Gillespie was born in Long Branch, New York, and grew up in New York City. A talented dancer, she worked in a chorus line at the Apollo Theater in Harlem and on the TOBA circuit, a group of black theaters in major cities across the East, Midwest, and South.

Upon meeting Lorraine in 1937, Gillespie was immediately captivated by her beauty. Unlike many of her fellow dancers, Lorraine disliked hanging out in bars after work. She, instead, preferred to return to her hotel room to knit or read her Bible.

Lorraine turned down Dizzy the first few times he asked her out. A friend finally convinced her that Dizzy was a good guy and she agreed to date him. They married in 1940 and made their first home together in Queens, New York, where Lorraine ran a tap-dance studio. They moved to Englewood, New Jersey, in 1965 and lived there until Dizzy's death in 1993.

Lorraine managed her husband's business and personal affairs and did her best to keep him away from the temptations of drugs and alcohol. Dizzy often praised her financial skills. "Lorraine knows how to handle money," he said. "Without her, I wouldn't have a quarter."[2]

When Lorraine died at age 84 in 2004, Dizzy's cousin Marion Frazier told the Associated Press that the Gillespies' relationship was built on love and trust. "She was good for him mentally and physically and spiritually as well," Frazier said. "She made sure that he went [sic] the right road and not the wrong road."[3]

Chapter **4**

Bop, Brawls, and Big Bands

Gillespie had been playing with Cab Calloway for two years when trumpeter Jonah Jones joined the band in 1941. The hiring upset Gillespie, who had enjoyed his position as the band's primary soloist. Suddenly the show was being rewritten and Jones was getting the spotlight. Gillespie became even angrier when Calloway asked Jones to join the Cab Jivers, a quintet within the larger Calloway band.

Gillespie resorted to pulling childish pranks on his fellow musicians and disrespected Calloway by shooting spitballs across the stage during live performances. In September 1941, the feud between Gillespie and Calloway grew violent. In the middle of a show at the State Theatre in Hartford, Connecticut, Jonah Jones started throwing spitballs at the group's drummer. The incident enraged Calloway, who immediately accused Gillespie—who this time was innocent. The more Gillespie denied his guilt, the angrier Calloway became, until he finally grabbed the trumpet player. Gillespie, both shocked and insulted, swiped at Calloway with a knife.

Gillespie's band mates tried to break up the fight, but before they could, Gillespie sliced into Calloway's rear end—a wound that required ten stitches. Gillespie was fired.

Gillespie then freelanced around New York, playing with and arranging music for many bands, including those of Coleman Hawkins,

Benny Carter, Earl Hines, Ella Fitzgerald, Duke Ellington, Charlie Barnet, and Lucky Millinder.

While playing with Millinder, Gillespie recorded a bop solo within the swing band song "Little John Special." After his solo, the band played a riff that Gillespie later developed into his own composition, "Salt Peanuts." In 1944, Gillespie made his first small-group bop recordings. Some were performed with Coleman Hawkins' band, and others, including "Salt Peanuts" and "Hot House," were recorded under his own name with Charlie "Yardbird" Parker.

In the early 1940s, Gillespie led a small band with Oscar Pettiford and worked as music director for a big band led by Billy Eckstine. In early 1945, Gillespie started his own big band. The band was a financial failure, so Gillespie abandoned it and, in November 1945, formed a bop quintet—which later grew to be a sextet—with Parker.

Gillespie really wanted to lead a big band, so he gave it another try in 1946. The new band worked to weave Afro-Cuban rhythms with American jazz and, at different times, included such prominent musicians as J. J. Johnson, Sonny Stitt, James Moody, Jimmy Heath, and John Coltrane. In 1947, Gillespie decided to add a Cuban percussionist to his big band. Conga player Chano Pozo collaborated with Gillespie on a series of recordings that are among the earliest examples of Latin jazz. "Cubano Be, Cubano Bop" was written by George Russell, specifically to showcase Pozo's skills. That piece and "Manteca" are notable examples of the ways in which Gillespie strived to blend Latin music and jazz.

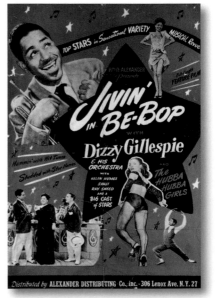

By 1950, Gillespie was in so much debt that he had to give up the big band. A year later, he and Dave Usher formed a record company called Dee Gee. Though the company was poorly financed and closed after just two and a half years, it produced several important works and introduced music lovers to future stars Kenny Burrell and Wynton Kelly.

In spring 1952, Gillespie accepted an invitation to perform as a soloist in an international jazz festival in Paris and at concerts in Holland and Belgium. Gillespie, wearing a plaid beret, was a hit with Paris audiences. Their appreciation inspired him to head into the recording studio. Over the course of just three weeks, he recorded 32 singles for the French labels Blue Star and Vogue.

Charles Delaunay tried to convince Gillespie to stay in Paris a month or two longer, or perhaps to move there permanently. Delaunay was a popular French author, jazz expert, record producer, and co-founder of the Hot Club de France. He promised to make Gillespie an even bigger sensation. Lorraine didn't care about her husband's European popularity. Adamantly opposed to such a move, she told Dizzy to come home right away. He did.

Back in North America, the New Jazz Society, a group of Canadian music lovers, decided to produce an all-star quintet concert on May 15, 1953, at Toronto's Massey Hall. When Gillespie, Parker, Budd Powell, Max Roach, and Charles Mingus arrived for what was supposed to be a big show, they learned that only 700 tickets had been sold in the 2,765-seat auditorium. The musicians were disappointed, but nonetheless performed with unbridled enthusiasm and skill. Unfortunately, show organizers had more ideas than money. Gillespie walked away

William Gottlieb was a long-time music columnist for *The Washington Post*. He also worked as a photographer, taking portraits of prominent jazz musicians throughout his career, including this 1947 portrait of (left to right) Dave Lambert, John Simmons, Chubby Jackson, George Handy, and Dizzy Gillespie.

Ella Fitzgerald, known as the "First Lady of Song," sings to the accompaniment of Dizzy Gillespie, Ray Brown, Milt Jackson, and Timmie Rosenkrantz.

from "one of the most celebrated events in jazz history"[1] without earning a dime.

Shortly after the Massey Hall show, Lorraine convinced Dizzy it was in his best interests—at least businesswise—to accept an offer from concert promoter and record producer Norman Granz. By recording for his labels and touring just three months per year with Granz's Jazz at the Philharmonic (JATP) troupes, Gillespie was making more money than he'd made in a year with his own group. Granz could also provide Gillespie with almost limitless opportunities to record. Gillespie had sixteen recording sessions in 1954 and 1955.

After several years leading small groups, Gillespie accepted a 1956 invitation from New York Congressman Adam Clayton Powell to form a racially integrated band to serve as cultural ambassadors for the United States. The thought was that Gillespie's soothing music would go a long way toward easing tensions during a nuclear crisis. Gillespie and his hand-selected big band traveled and performed in Iran, Lebanon, Syria, Pakistan, Turkey, Greece, Africa, Yugoslavia, and South America. Wherever they traveled, the musicians made a point of performing with local bands. The experience made an impact with both the American artists and their audiences.

Gillespie kept this band together for two years, but when government funding ran out, he was unable to continue paying the salaries and travel costs associated with such a large ensemble. In 1958, he returned to leading small groups.

Blowfish Cheeks and a Bent Trumpet

The longer Dizzy Gillespie played, the odder his appearance became. "My cheeks started bulging out," he wrote in his memoir, *To Be, or Not . . . To Bop.* "I didn't get any physical pain from it, but all of a sudden I looked like a frog whenever I played."[2]

NASA physicians wanted to X-ray Gillespie's cheeks to learn why they ballooned the way they did. Gillespie skipped his appointment, so the medical cause for his misshapen jowls was never officially documented.

The reason for his bent trumpet is less mysterious: Many of Dizzy and Lorraine's friends gathered at a club on January 6, 1953, to celebrate Lorraine's birthday. Dizzy stepped out to do an interview; when he returned, he discovered his pals had been goofing around on the bandstand. One of the men had fallen onto Gillespie's horn, bending the bell.

Not wanting to disrupt Lorraine's party, Gillespie picked up the deformed trumpet and started playing. The musician detected a subtle difference in the sounds that came from the instrument; he could play it softer and, because the bell was closer to his ear, he was hearing notes a split-second sooner.

Gillespie had his trumpet repaired the next day, but soon decided he preferred the bent version. He contacted the Martin Band Instrument Company and asked them to build a trumpet with a bell at a 45-degree angle. They made the horn to Gillespie's specifications, and he played one liked it throughout the rest of his career—bulging cheeks and all.

Chapter **5**

His Share of Controversies

That Dizzy Gillespie was a great musician is an undisputable fact. It would be untruthful, though, to present the story of his life as if it contained no controversies or conflicts.

His berets, fezzes, shades, and constant jive talking made him the ultimate hipster. The same showboating, need-for-the-spotlight antics that appealed to fans often annoyed and angered his band mates. Many fellow musicians resented his clowning around and disliked that his behavior stole attention from them.

Gillespie's bad behavior was not limited to the stage. He drank, used drugs, and dated other women while he was married to Lorraine. He even had a baby with one of those women: daughter Jeanie Bryson was born in 1958. He denied she was his child for many years but eventually acknowledged her as his. (She would go on to become a jazz singer and honor her father with a collection of songs, *The Dizzy Songbook,* for what would have been his ninetieth birthday.)

In 1956, President Dwight D. Eisenhower decided that Gillespie's strengths outweighed these well-known controversies. He asked

Gillespie to join a jazz tour aimed to ease tensions between the United States and the Soviet Union.

"President Eisenhower was deeply concerned about the country's image and how the U.S. was being portrayed," said Penny Von Eschen, a professor of history and American culture at the University of Michigan. "The U.S. was attempting to project itself as the leader of the free world, but many people in the world saw it as a culturally backward country."[1] Additionally, U.S. leaders worried that the nation's growing racial divide was hurting its international image.

"They basically said we've got to try and do something to show the world that America is progressing. And jazz seemed to be the answer to their dreams," Von Eschen told the (Memphis) *Commercial Appeal.*[2]

Gillespie and fellow black musicians Duke Ellington and Louis Armstrong joined white jazz greats Benny Goodman and Dave Brubeck to tour the world, spreading goodwill.

As the 1960s dawned, jazz became less symbolic of America's music scene and the world jazz tours shut down. At the same time, U.S. music fans were falling in love with rock and roll and out of love with jazz.

Jazz didn't go away, but music promoters and record producers were no longer willing to spend much money or effort on recordings. Jazz artists struggled to make a living, playing shows at small clubs and festivals. The difficult travel schedule, along with continuing racial unrest in the United States, made this time stressful for Gillespie.

In 1968, Gillespie converted from Christianity to the Baha'i faith. The teachings of the Baha'i emphasize peace and racial and religious unity. His new faith inspired him to give up alcohol and approach music—and life—with more spiritual guidance.

This sober and more spiritually centered Gillespie received another shot at success when his longtime associate Norman Granz established Pablo Records in 1973. The label was dedicated to producing artists Granz considered legendary but who, often because of their age, were being overlooked by other studios. Gillespie made several landmark recordings for Granz, including *Dizzy's Big 4* and *Oscar Peterson and Dizzy Gillespie.*

Dizzy Gillespie plays with
the Giants of Jazz, a jazz
all-star group of the
1970s, during a show in
Hamburg, Germany.

Gillespie continued to perform and record extensively with his various small groups into the late 1980s. In 1977, he organized a jazz cruise to Cuba, breaking the United States' seventeen-year ban on travel to the island. There, he collaborated with local musicians, including saxophonist Paquito D'Rivera and trumpeter Arturo Sandoval. Both of these men later immigrated to the United States, where they continued to perform with Gillespie.

In 1978, Gillespie even managed to convince a U.S. president to participate in a public performance of his classic song "Salt Peanuts." Gillespie was at the White House for the twenty-fifth anniversary of the Newport Jazz Festival, and President Jimmy Carter (a former peanut farmer) requested the song. Gillespie agreed to play it, but only if Carter

In 1978, President Jimmy Carter, left, sang on stage while Dizzy Gillespie and drummer Max Roach played "Salt Peanuts."

would sing. The president did, and the performance was broadcast to the world.

As Gillespie got older, he welcomed the opportunity to share his expertise with younger, less experienced musicians, often inviting them to join him onstage for live performances. Among the many musicians whom Gillespie mentored were trumpeters Jon Faddis, Sandoval, and D'Rivera, and pianist Danilo Pérez and trombonist Steve Turre.

In 1988, Gillespie put together his last big band. The United Nation Orchestra, named in honor of the Baha'i belief in the unity of all mankind, brought together many of the best jazz musicians from the United States and Latin America. It was an ensemble that celebrated the multicultural ideal that drove much of Gillespie's career. In 1989, at the Royal Festival Hall in London, he directed the band in a concert that is often recalled for its spectacular rendition of Gillespie's "A Night in Tunisia."

In honor of his seventy-fifth birthday, Gillespie performed for one month at New York's famed Blue Note jazz club. Although he had to be helped on stage, Gillespie joked around and played several improvisational trumpet solos that awed critics. A *New York Times* reviewer wrote about Gillespie's performance: "As usual, he was his witty amiable self, in command of both the audience and his trumpet."[3] Several albums were produced from recordings made at those shows, including *To Bird with Love.*

Gillespie capped off his yearlong birthday celebration with a Caribbean cruise featuring a sixty-member all-star jazz band. Lorraine joined him for the jam session at sea.

On January 6, 1993, just ten weeks after returning from his birthday cruise, Gillespie died in his sleep at an Englewood, New Jersey, hospital, where he was being treated for pancreatic cancer. According to his wishes, he was given a private funeral in the Baha'i tradition, as well as a public service at the Cathedral of St. John the Divine, both in New York City. Gillespie is buried at the Flushing Cemetery in Queens, New York. His death marked the end of his sixty-year career as a musical innovator, mentor, and cultural ambassador.

Singer Tony Bennett joins Dizzy Gillespie on stage during a series of concerts at New York City's Blue Note night club. The shows were in celebration of Gillespie's seventy-fifth birthday.

"I never looked behind me to find out what other people were playing or doing," Gillespie told a *New York Times* reporter in the 1980s. "I just keep going, looking for new ideas, practicing. Even 'A Night in Tunisia' doesn't bore me; I'm never bored. There's always a new way to play anything."[4]

That eagerness to adapt and experiment, combined with musical prowess and persistence, made John Birks "Dizzy" Gillespie one of America's greatest contributors to modern jazz.

Swinging the Vote

In the mid-1960s, Gillespie's booking agency printed buttons that said "Dizzy Gillespie for President" as a way to promote their artist and sell albums. As civil rights issues heated up, though, Gillespie stepped beyond the gag and launched an official challenge to incumbent Lyndon B. Johnson and Republican nominee Barry Goldwater in the 1964 presidential election.

Over the years, many have suggested that Gillespie was never serious about running for president. They believed his candidacy was just a publicity stunt run by jazz critic Ralph Gleason, his wife Jean Gleason, and longtime fan Ramona Crowell. Stunt or not, The John Birks Society was organized to campaign on his behalf and was active in twenty-five states. The group successfully petitioned to get Gillespie's name on the presidential ballot in California.

The musician developed a political platform, drawing attention to issues of race and discrimination. Other items on his agenda included providing free education and health care to all and sending a black astronaut to the moon (if none could be found, Dizzy offered to go himself).

If elected, he also promised to rename the White House the "Blues House." For the presidential cabinet, he proposed changing the stuffy title of secretary to minister. His cabinet would include jazz greats Duke Ellington as minister of state, Max Roach as minister of defense, Charles Mingus as minister of peace, Peggy Lee as minister of labor, and Miles Davis as the director of the CIA.

In the end, Gillespie withdrew from the race, and Johnson was elected to a second term.

1917 John Birks Gillespie is born in Cheraw, South Carolina, on October 21.

1927 John's father dies.

1928 John decides he wants to make his mother proud by becoming a musician.

1929 In fifth grade, John joins the Robert Smalls School band. He plays trombone. Shortly after, he takes music lessons from his cousin Norman Powe and starts playing trumpet.

1933 He graduates from the Robert Smalls School and, with the help of Catherine McKay, attends North Carolina's Laurinburg Institute with Norman.

1935 He moves to Philadelphia to be with his family; he joins the musician's union. While Gillespie is working with Frankie Fairfax's big band, Fats Palmer gives him the nickname Dizzy.

1937 Gillespie moves to New York City. He is hired to play with Teddy Hill's band, which tours the United States and Europe. He meets Lorraine Willis.

1939 After the New York World's Fair, Teddy Hill's band breaks up. Gillespie begins playing for Cab Calloway.

1940 Gillespie and Lorraine Willis marry.

1941 Calloway fires Gillespie after Gillespie sinks a knife into Calloway's buttocks.

1944 Gillespie receives New Star Award from *Esquire* magazine.

1945 He starts his own band, but it fails. With Charlie Parker, he forms a successful bop quintet.

1952 After a well-received jazz festival in Paris, Gillespie records 32 singles for French record labels.

1956 With a racially integrated band serving as musical ambassadors, Gillespie performs in Iran, Lebanon, Syria, Pakistan, Turkey, Greece, Africa, Yugoslavia, and South America. Later that year, he joins a jazz tour aimed to ease tensions between the United States and the Soviet Union.

1958 His daughter, Jeanie Bryson, is born.

1959 In Cheraw, South Carolina, Gillespie performs at the first integrated concert in a U.S. public school.

1964 Gillespie runs for president against Lyndon B. Johnson and Barry Goldwater.

1968 He converts from Christianity to the Baha'i faith.

1972 He receives the Handel Medallion from the City of New York and the Paul Robeson Award from Rutgers University Institute of Jazz Studies.

1977	He organizes a jazz cruise to Cuba—the first time Americans have traveled to that country in seventeen years. He performs for President Jimmy Carter and the Shah of Iran at the White House.
1978	He performs "Salt Peanuts" with President Carter at a White House jazz concert.
1982	Gillespie is inducted into the Big Band and Jazz Hall of Fame.
1989	He receives the Lifetime Achievement Award from the National Association of Recording Arts and Sciences.
1989	At Royal Festival Hall in London, he directs the band in a spectacular rendition of "Night in Tunisia." Gillespie receives the National Medal of Arts; the Duke Ellington Award from the Society of Composers, Authors and Publishers; and the Grammy Lifetime Achievement Award.
1990	He receives a Kennedy Center Honor.
1992	He plays at New York's Blue Note to celebrate his seventy-fifth birthday, and continues to celebrate with a sixty-member band on a Caribbean cruise.
1993	On January 6, Gillespie dies from complications of pancreatic cancer.
1998	The Dizzy Gillespie™ All-Star Big Band, a group of world-class jazz musicians, is formed to perform Dizzy Gillespie's music and to continue his legacy.
2007	Jeanie Bryson honors her father with a collection of songs called *The Dizzy Songbook*.
2012	Award-winning jazz trumpeter Arturo Sandoval stages a series of tribute concerts billed as "A Tribute to My Friend Dizzy Gillespie."

1937 *Teddy Hill and His NBC Orchestra* (Bluebird)

1939 *Lionel Hampton and His Orchestra* (Victor)

1940 *Cab Calloway and His Orchestra* (Vocalion)

1945 *Dizzy Gillespie Sextet* (Manor in January; Guild/Musicraft in March; Guild in May)

   Charlie Parker's Ree Boppers (Savoy)

1946 *Dizzy Gillespie's Jazzmen* (Dial)

   Dizzy Gillespie Sextet (Musicraft)

1947 *Dizzy Gillespie and His Orchestra* (Victor)

1948 *Dizzy Gillespie and His Orchestra* (Gene Norman Presents)

1952 *Dizzy Gillespie and the Cool Jazz Stars* (MGM)

1953 *Quintet of the Year—Jazz at Massey Hall* (Debut)

   Dizzy Gillespie All-Stars (Broadcast)

1956 *Dizzy Gillespie's All-Stars—For Musicians Only* (Verve)

1957 *Dizzy Gillespie at Newport* (Verve)

1959 *Have Trumpet, Will Excite!* (Verve)

   The Ebullient Mr. Gillespie (Verve)

1961 *An Electrifying Evening with the Dizzy Gillespie Quintet* (Verve)

1962 *Dizzy on the Riviera* (Philips)

1964 *Jambo Caribe* (Limelight)

1968 *Dizzy Gillespie Reunion Big Band In Berlin* (SABA)

1973 *The Giant* (Prestige)

1974 *Oscar Peterson and Dizzy Gillespie* (Pablo)

1975 *Dizzy Gillespie y Machito: Afro-Cuban Jazz Moods* (Pablo)

   Jazz Maturity . . . Where It's Coming From (OJC)

1976 *Dizzy's Party* (OJC)

1977 *Count Basie and Dizzy Gillespie: The Gifted Ones* (Pablo)

1989 *Dizzy Gillespie Live at the Royal Festival Hall* (BBC)

1992 *Groovin' High—A Compilation* (Savoy)

   To Bird With Love (Telarc)

1997 *Diz 'n' Bird—Recordings from Charlie Parker and Dizzy Gillespie's 1947 Show at Carnegie Hall* (Blue Note)

Chapter 1. A Turbulent Childhood

1. Donald L. Maggin, *Dizzy: The Life and Times of John Birks Gillespie* (New York: HarperEntertainment, 2005), p. 5.
2. Dizzy Gillespie and Al Fraser, *To Be, or Not . . . To Bop: Memoirs* (Garden City, NY: Doubleday, 1979), p. 30.
3. Maggin, p. 5.
4. Peter Galuszka, "NCAA Scrutiny Helps Hasten Decline of Tradition-Rich Black Prep School," *Diverse: Issues in Higher Education,* May 10, 2010, http://diverseeducation.com/article/13774c1/ncaa-scrutiny-helps-hasten-decline-of-tradition-rich-black-prep-school.html

Chapter 2. Making a Name for Himself

1. Dizzy Gillespie and Al Fraser, *To Be, or Not . . . To Bop: Memoirs* (Garden City, NY: Doubleday, 1979), p. 49.
2. Ibid.
3. Ibid., pp. 54–55.

Chapter 3. The Birth of Bebop

1. Donald L. Maggin, *Dizzy: The Life and Times of John Birks Gillespie* (New York: HarperEntertainment, 2005), p. 98.
2. Robin D. G. Kelley, "The Jazz Wife: Muse and Manager," *The New York Times,* July 21, 2002, http://www.nytimes.com/2002/07/21/arts/music-the-jazz-wife-muse-and-manager.html?pagewanted=all&src=pm
3. "Lorraine Willis Gillespie, Widow of Jazz Legend," *The Associated Press,* June 16, 2004, http://www.newsday.com/news/lorraine-willis-gillespie-widow-of-jazz-legend-1.738607

Chapter 4. Bop, Brawls, and Big Bands

1. Donald L. Maggin, *Dizzy: The Life and Times of John Birks Gillespie* (New York: HarperEntertainment, 2005), p. 55.
2. Dizzy Gillespie and Al Fraser. *To Be, or Not . . . To Bop: Memoirs* (Garden City, NY: Doubleday, 1979), p. 315.

Chapter 5. His Share of Controversies

1. Bob Mehr, "Pied Pipers of Jazz—Images Capture U.S. Giants on Goodwill Tours Abroad." *Commercial Appeal* [Memphis], July 30, 2010, http://commercial-appeal.vlex.com/vid/pied-pipers-capture-goodwill-tours-abroad-215001891
2. Ibid.
3. Peter Watrous, "Dizzy Gillespie, Who Sounded Some of Modern Jazz's Earliest Notes, Dies at 75," *The New York Times,* January 7, 1993, http://www.nytimes.com/learning/general/onthisday/bday/1021.html
4. Peter Watrous, "Pop View; Dizzy Gillespie: More Than the Man with the Bent Horn." *The New York Times,* January 17, 1993. http://www.nytimes.com/1993/01/17/arts/pop-view-dizzy-gillespie-more-than-the-man-with-the-bent-horn.html?pagewanted=all&src=pm

alma mater (ALL-muh MAH-ter)—Any school, college, or university that one has attended.

amateur (AM-uh-chur)—A person who plays music or a sport just for fun rather than as a profession.

asthma (AZ-muh)—A potentially fatal lung disorder in which airways begin to close, making breathing difficult; sufferers often cough, wheeze, and feel tightness in their chest.

Baha'i (bah-HY)—Having to do with Bahaism, a belief system that values all religions equally and that stresses universal brotherhood and social equality.

boll (BAHL)—The pod of a plant, such as cotton.

cornet (kor-NET)—A brass instrument similar to but smaller than a trumpet.

extravaganza (ek-straa-vah-GAN-zah)—A spectacular show or event.

freelancing (FREE-lant-sing)—Working on a per-job basis, without a long-term commitment with an employer.

improvisational (im-prah-veh-ZAY-shuh-nul)—Playing or composing music on the spot, without preparation.

intricate (IN-trih-kit)—Having fancy parts or elements.

jazz (JAZ)—A type of music that has a strong, lively beat and for which players often make up musical phrases on the spot.

Lindy Hopper—A person who performed an energetic American dance popular in the 1930s. The Lindy was a blend of many other dances, including tap and the Charleston.

lynch (LINCH)—To put to death (often by hanging) by mob action and without the legal order of a judge or jury.

minstrel (MIN-strul)—An entertainer who usually performs music, poetry, or jokes.

quintet (kwin-TET)—A musical group of five individuals.

riff—A relatively simple, repeated musical phrase.

scat (SKAT)—Improvised singing using nonsense syllables.

stroke (STOHK)—A brain injury caused by a blockage or rupture of a blood vessel to the brain; symptoms may include loss of muscle control, dizziness, and slurred speech.

sustain (suh-STAYN)—In music, to steadily hold or maintain a tone.

unison (YOO-nih-sun)—In music, to play in harmony and at the same time

valet (vah-LAY)—An employee who takes care of clothing and other personal items.

About the Author

Mary Boone has written more than two dozen books for young readers, including biographies about musicians *Pink, 50 Cent, Akon,* and Kids Can Cook: *Midwestern Recipes.* She took years and years of piano and organ lessons but still considers herself a very "average" musician. She, her husband Mitch, and their kids, Eve and Eli, live in Tacoma, Washington.